50 Premium Island Dessert Recipes for Home

By: Kelly Johnson

Table of Contents

- Coconut Pineapple Upside-Down Cake
- Mango Sticky Rice
- Rum-Soaked Banana Fritters
- Passion Fruit Cheesecake
- Guava and Cream Cheese Tart
- Pineapple Coconut Sorbet
- Spiced Plantain Cake
- Tropical Fruit Pavlova
- Key Lime Pie
- Coconut Macaroons
- Chocolate-Covered Pineapple Bites
- Jamaican Rum Cake
- Mango-Lime Tart
- Pineapple Coconut Panna Cotta
- Banana Rum Bread Pudding
- Tropical Fruit Salad with Mint
- Coconut Almond Bars
- Passion Fruit Mousse
- Papaya and Lime Granita
- Banana Foster
- Coconut Cream Pie
- Pineapple Coconut Cupcakes
- Guava Sorbet
- Tropical Tiramisu
- Mango Chia Seed Pudding
- Pineapple Upside-Down Cupcakes
- Coconut Pineapple Bread
- Rum and Raisin Rice Pudding
- Spiced Apple and Coconut Crumble
- Passion Fruit Jelly
- Tropical Fruit Tartlets
- Key Lime Bars

- Coconut Banana Smoothie Bowl
- Pineapple Coconut Rice Pudding
- Mango and Coconut Ice Cream
- Pineapple Rum Flan
- Coconut Chocolate Truffles
- Mango and Pineapple Pavlova
- Tropical Fruit Sorbet
- Rum-Soaked Coconut Cake
- Guava Cream Cheese Muffins
- Pineapple and Coconut Cheesecake Bars
- Banana Coconut Muffins
- Passion Fruit Sorbet with Fresh Mint
- Tropical Fruit Parfait
- Coconut-Lime Bars
- Mango-Pineapple Cupcakes
- Pineapple Coconut Bars
- Spiced Banana Cake with Rum Glaze
- Coconut-Pineapple Macarons

Coconut Pineapple Upside-Down Cake

Ingredients:

For the Topping:

- 1/4 cup unsalted butter
- 1/2 cup brown sugar
- 6-8 pineapple rings (fresh or canned)
- Maraschino cherries (optional, for garnish)
- 1/2 cup shredded coconut

For the Cake:

- 1 1/2 cups all-purpose flour
- 1 cup granulated sugar
- 1/2 cup unsalted butter, softened
- 1/2 cup coconut milk
- 2 large eggs
- 1 1/2 tsp baking powder
- 1/4 tsp salt
- 1/2 tsp vanilla extract
- 1/2 tsp coconut extract (optional)

Instructions:

1. **Prepare the Topping:**
   - Preheat your oven to 350°F (175°C).
   - In a small saucepan, melt 1/4 cup butter over medium heat. Stir in brown sugar and cook until dissolved.
   - Pour the butter-sugar mixture into the bottom of a 9-inch round cake pan.
   - Arrange pineapple rings over the sugar mixture. Place a maraschino cherry in the center of each pineapple ring if using. Sprinkle shredded coconut over the top.
2. **Make the Cake Batter:**
   - In a medium bowl, whisk together flour, baking powder, and salt.
   - In a large bowl, cream together 1/2 cup softened butter and granulated sugar until light and fluffy.
   - Beat in eggs one at a time, then mix in vanilla extract and coconut extract.
   - Gradually add flour mixture to the butter mixture, alternating with coconut milk. Begin and end with flour mixture.
3. **Assemble and Bake:**
   - Pour the cake batter evenly over the prepared pineapple topping in the cake pan.
   - Smooth the top with a spatula.

- Bake for 35-40 minutes, or until a toothpick inserted into the center comes out clean.

4. **Cool and Serve:**
    - Let the cake cool in the pan for 10 minutes, then invert onto a serving plate. Carefully remove the cake pan.
    - Serve warm or at room temperature. Enjoy your tropical treat!

Mango Sticky Rice

Ingredients:

For the Sticky Rice:

- 1 cup Thai sticky rice (also called glutinous rice)
- 1 1/4 cups water
- 1 cup coconut milk
- 1/2 cup granulated sugar
- 1/4 tsp salt

For the Mango:

- 2 ripe mangoes, peeled, pitted, and sliced

For Garnish:

- 2 tbsp toasted sesame seeds or toasted coconut (optional)
- Fresh mint leaves (optional)

Instructions:

1. **Prepare the Sticky Rice:**
   - Rinse the sticky rice under cold water until the water runs clear. Soak the rice in a bowl of water for at least 1 hour, or overnight if possible.
   - Drain the rice and place it in a steamer basket lined with cheesecloth or parchment paper. Steam the rice over simmering water for about 20-25 minutes, or until tender.
2. **Make the Coconut Sauce:**
   - While the rice is steaming, in a small saucepan, combine coconut milk, granulated sugar, and salt.
   - Heat over medium heat, stirring occasionally, until the sugar is dissolved. Do not let it boil. Remove from heat and set aside.
3. **Combine Rice and Coconut Sauce:**
   - Once the rice is cooked, transfer it to a large bowl.
   - Pour about 3/4 cup of the coconut sauce over the hot rice. Stir gently to combine, making sure the rice is evenly coated. Let it sit for about 15 minutes to absorb the coconut sauce.
4. **Serve:**
   - To serve, spoon a portion of the sticky rice onto individual plates or bowls.
   - Top with slices of fresh mango.
   - Drizzle with additional coconut sauce if desired.

    - Garnish with toasted sesame seeds or toasted coconut, and fresh mint leaves if using.

Enjoy your delicious Mango Sticky Rice!

Rum-Soaked Banana Fritters

Ingredients:

For the Rum-Soaked Bananas:

- 4 ripe bananas, peeled and sliced
- 1/4 cup dark rum
- 2 tbsp brown sugar

For the Fritter Batter:

- 1 cup all-purpose flour
- 1/4 cup cornstarch
- 2 tbsp granulated sugar
- 1/2 tsp baking powder
- 1/4 tsp baking soda
- 1/4 tsp salt
- 1/2 cup cold sparkling water (or cold water)
- 1 large egg

For Frying:

- Vegetable oil (for frying)

For Serving:

- Powdered sugar (for dusting)
- Honey or caramel sauce (optional)

Instructions:

1. **Soak the Bananas:**
    - In a medium bowl, combine sliced bananas, dark rum, and brown sugar. Toss to coat the bananas evenly.
    - Let the bananas soak in the rum mixture for at least 15 minutes, or up to 1 hour for more flavor.
2. **Prepare the Fritter Batter:**
    - In a large bowl, whisk together flour, cornstarch, granulated sugar, baking powder, baking soda, and salt.
    - In a separate bowl, beat the egg and then add the cold sparkling water.
    - Pour the wet ingredients into the dry ingredients and stir until just combined. The batter will be slightly lumpy, which is okay.
3. **Fry the Fritters:**

- Heat about 2 inches of vegetable oil in a deep skillet or heavy pan over medium-high heat to 350°F (175°C).
- Using a fork or tongs, dip rum-soaked banana slices into the batter, allowing any excess to drip off.
- Carefully drop the coated banana slices into the hot oil. Fry in batches, making sure not to overcrowd the pan.
- Fry for 2-3 minutes per side, or until golden brown and crispy.
- Use a slotted spoon to remove the fritters from the oil and place them on paper towels to drain.

4. **Serve:**
    - Dust the hot fritters with powdered sugar.
    - Serve warm, with a drizzle of honey or caramel sauce if desired.

Enjoy your delicious Rum-Soaked Banana Fritters!

Passion Fruit Cheesecake

Ingredients:

For the Crust:

- 1 1/2 cups graham cracker crumbs
- 1/4 cup granulated sugar
- 1/2 cup unsalted butter, melted

For the Filling:

- 4 (8 oz) packages cream cheese, softened
- 1 cup granulated sugar
- 4 large eggs
- 1 cup sour cream
- 1 cup passion fruit juice (fresh or bottled)
- 1 tsp vanilla extract

For the Topping:

- 1/2 cup passion fruit pulp or puree (fresh or canned)
- 1/4 cup granulated sugar
- 1 tbsp water or lemon juice

Instructions:

1. **Prepare the Crust:**
    - Preheat your oven to 325°F (163°C).
    - In a medium bowl, mix graham cracker crumbs, granulated sugar, and melted butter until combined.
    - Press the mixture firmly into the bottom of a 9-inch springform pan to form an even layer.
    - Bake for 10 minutes, then remove from the oven and let cool.
2. **Prepare the Filling:**
    - In a large bowl, beat cream cheese with an electric mixer until smooth and creamy.
    - Gradually add granulated sugar and beat until combined.
    - Add eggs one at a time, mixing well after each addition.
    - Mix in sour cream, passion fruit juice, and vanilla extract until smooth.
3. **Bake the Cheesecake:**
    - Pour the cream cheese mixture over the cooled crust in the springform pan.
    - Smooth the top with a spatula.
    - Bake for 50-60 minutes, or until the edges are set and the center is slightly jiggly.

- Turn off the oven and let the cheesecake cool in the oven with the door slightly open for 1 hour.
- Refrigerate the cheesecake for at least 4 hours, or overnight.
4. **Prepare the Topping:**
    - In a small saucepan, combine passion fruit pulp, granulated sugar, and water or lemon juice.
    - Heat over medium heat, stirring occasionally, until the sugar is dissolved and the mixture thickens slightly, about 5 minutes.
    - Let the topping cool to room temperature.
5. **Serve:**
    - Spread or drizzle the passion fruit topping over the chilled cheesecake.
    - Slice and serve.

Enjoy your delightful Passion Fruit Cheesecake!

Guava and Cream Cheese Tart

Ingredients:

For the Crust:

- 1 1/2 cups graham cracker crumbs
- 1/4 cup granulated sugar
- 1/2 cup unsalted butter, melted

For the Filling:

- 8 oz cream cheese, softened
- 1/2 cup granulated sugar
- 1 large egg
- 1/2 cup sour cream
- 1 tsp vanilla extract
- 1/2 cup guava paste, cut into small cubes (or guava jam/puree)

For the Guava Glaze (Optional):

- 1/4 cup guava paste
- 2 tbsp water

Instructions:

1. **Prepare the Crust:**
    - Preheat your oven to 350°F (175°C).
    - In a medium bowl, mix graham cracker crumbs, granulated sugar, and melted butter until well combined.
    - Press the mixture evenly into the bottom and up the sides of a 9-inch tart pan to form the crust.
    - Bake for 8-10 minutes, or until the crust is lightly golden. Remove from the oven and let cool.
2. **Prepare the Filling:**
    - In a large bowl, beat softened cream cheese with granulated sugar until smooth and creamy.
    - Add the egg and mix until fully incorporated.
    - Stir in sour cream and vanilla extract until smooth.
    - Gently fold in the guava paste cubes or guava jam/puree.
3. **Assemble and Bake:**
    - Pour the cream cheese filling into the cooled tart crust, spreading it evenly.
    - Bake for 25-30 minutes, or until the filling is set and slightly puffed.

- Remove from the oven and let cool to room temperature, then refrigerate for at least 2 hours to set.
4. **Prepare the Guava Glaze (Optional):**
    - In a small saucepan, combine guava paste and water.
    - Heat over low heat, stirring occasionally, until the guava paste melts and the mixture is smooth.
    - Let the glaze cool slightly.
5. **Serve:**
    - Once the tart is chilled and set, spread or drizzle the guava glaze over the top if using.
    - Garnish with fresh mint or fruit slices if desired.
    - Slice and serve.

Enjoy your delicious Guava and Cream Cheese Tart!

Pineapple Coconut Sorbet

Ingredients:

- 2 cups fresh pineapple chunks (or canned pineapple, drained)
- 1 cup coconut milk
- 1/2 cup granulated sugar
- 1/4 cup lime juice (freshly squeezed)
- 1/2 tsp vanilla extract
- 1/4 tsp salt

Instructions:

1. **Prepare the Pineapple:**
   - If using fresh pineapple, cut it into chunks and freeze for at least 2 hours. If using canned pineapple, drain and freeze it.
2. **Blend the Ingredients:**
   - In a blender or food processor, combine frozen pineapple chunks, coconut milk, granulated sugar, lime juice, vanilla extract, and salt.
   - Blend until smooth and creamy. You may need to stop and scrape down the sides to ensure everything is well combined.
3. **Chill the Mixture:**
   - Taste the mixture and adjust sweetness or lime juice if needed.
   - Pour the mixture into a shallow dish and freeze for about 2 hours, stirring every 30 minutes to break up ice crystals and ensure a smooth texture.
4. **Serve:**
   - Once the sorbet is fully frozen and has a scoopable consistency, use a spoon or ice cream scoop to serve.
   - Garnish with fresh mint or pineapple slices if desired.

Enjoy your refreshing Pineapple Coconut Sorbet!

Spiced Plantain Cake

Ingredients:

For the Cake:

- 3 ripe plantains, peeled and mashed (about 1 1/2 cups mashed)
- 1/2 cup unsalted butter, softened
- 1 cup granulated sugar
- 2 large eggs
- 1 tsp vanilla extract
- 1 1/2 cups all-purpose flour
- 1 tsp baking powder
- 1/2 tsp baking soda
- 1/2 tsp ground cinnamon
- 1/4 tsp ground nutmeg
- 1/4 tsp ground allspice
- 1/4 tsp salt
- 1/2 cup chopped nuts (e.g., walnuts or pecans) - optional

For the Glaze (optional):

- 1/2 cup powdered sugar
- 2-3 tbsp milk
- 1/4 tsp vanilla extract

Instructions:

1. **Prepare the Oven and Pan:**
    - Preheat your oven to 350°F (175°C).
    - Grease and flour a 9-inch round cake pan or line it with parchment paper.
2. **Make the Cake Batter:**
    - In a large bowl, cream together the softened butter and granulated sugar until light and fluffy.
    - Beat in the eggs one at a time, then mix in the vanilla extract.
    - In a separate bowl, whisk together the flour, baking powder, baking soda, cinnamon, nutmeg, allspice, and salt.
    - Gradually add the dry ingredients to the butter mixture, mixing just until combined.
    - Fold in the mashed plantains until evenly incorporated.
    - If using, fold in the chopped nuts.
3. **Bake the Cake:**
    - Pour the batter into the prepared cake pan and smooth the top.

- Bake for 30-35 minutes, or until a toothpick inserted into the center comes out clean.
- Allow the cake to cool in the pan for 10 minutes, then transfer it to a wire rack to cool completely.

4. **Prepare the Glaze (optional):**
    - In a small bowl, whisk together powdered sugar, milk, and vanilla extract until smooth and drizzleable.
    - Drizzle the glaze over the cooled cake if desired.
5. **Serve:**
    - Slice and enjoy your Spiced Plantain Cake!

This cake pairs wonderfully with a cup of tea or coffee. Enjoy!

Tropical Fruit Pavlova

Ingredients:

For the Meringue:

- 4 large egg whites
- 1 cup granulated sugar
- 1/2 tsp cream of tartar
- 1 tsp vanilla extract
- 1/2 tsp cornstarch
- 1 tbsp white vinegar

For the Topping:

- 1 cup heavy cream
- 2 tbsp powdered sugar
- 1 tsp vanilla extract
- 1 cup fresh tropical fruits, diced (such as mango, pineapple, kiwi, and passion fruit)
- Fresh mint leaves (for garnish, optional)

Instructions:

1. **Prepare the Meringue:**
    - Preheat your oven to 275°F (135°C) and line a baking sheet with parchment paper. Draw a 9-inch circle on the parchment as a guide, then flip it over so the ink is on the underside.
    - In a clean, dry mixing bowl, beat the egg whites with an electric mixer on medium speed until foamy.
    - Add the cream of tartar and continue beating until soft peaks form.
    - Gradually add the granulated sugar, 1 tablespoon at a time, beating on high speed until stiff, glossy peaks form.
    - Gently fold in the vanilla extract, cornstarch, and white vinegar.
    - Spoon the meringue onto the parchment paper, using the drawn circle as a guide. Spread it out and build up the sides to create a slight well in the center.
2. **Bake the Meringue:**
    - Bake the meringue for 1 hour to 1 hour 15 minutes, or until it is crisp and dry on the outside but still soft and marshmallowy inside.
    - Turn off the oven and let the meringue cool completely in the oven with the door slightly ajar.
3. **Prepare the Topping:**
    - In a medium bowl, whip the heavy cream with an electric mixer until soft peaks form.

- Add powdered sugar and vanilla extract, and continue to whip until stiff peaks form.
 - Gently fold in the diced tropical fruits.
4. **Assemble the Pavlova:**
 - Once the meringue is completely cool, carefully remove it from the parchment paper and place it on a serving platter.
 - Spread the whipped cream mixture over the meringue, filling the well in the center.
 - Top with additional tropical fruit and garnish with fresh mint leaves if desired.
5. **Serve:**
 - Slice and serve immediately. The Pavlova is best enjoyed fresh.

Enjoy your Tropical Fruit Pavlova!

Key Lime Pie

Ingredients:

For the Crust:

- 1 1/2 cups graham cracker crumbs
- 1/4 cup granulated sugar
- 1/2 cup unsalted butter, melted

For the Filling:

- 1 can (14 oz) sweetened condensed milk
- 1/2 cup fresh key lime juice (or regular lime juice)
- 3 large egg yolks
- Zest of 2 key limes (or 1 regular lime)

For the Topping:

- 1 cup heavy cream
- 2 tbsp powdered sugar
- 1/2 tsp vanilla extract
- Lime zest or lime slices (for garnish)

Instructions:

1. **Prepare the Crust:**
    - Preheat your oven to 350°F (175°C).
    - In a medium bowl, combine graham cracker crumbs, granulated sugar, and melted butter until the mixture resembles coarse sand.
    - Press the mixture evenly into the bottom and up the sides of a 9-inch pie pan.
    - Bake for 8-10 minutes, or until the crust is lightly golden. Remove from the oven and let it cool.
2. **Prepare the Filling:**
    - In a large bowl, whisk together sweetened condensed milk, key lime juice, egg yolks, and lime zest until smooth.
    - Pour the filling into the cooled graham cracker crust.
3. **Bake the Pie:**
    - Bake the pie at 350°F (175°C) for 15-20 minutes, or until the filling is set and the edges are slightly puffed.
    - Remove from the oven and let it cool to room temperature, then refrigerate for at least 3 hours or until fully chilled.
4. **Prepare the Topping:**

- In a medium bowl, whip the heavy cream with an electric mixer until soft peaks form.
   - Add powdered sugar and vanilla extract, and continue to whip until stiff peaks form.
5. **Assemble and Serve:**
   - Spread or pipe the whipped cream over the chilled pie.
   - Garnish with additional lime zest or lime slices if desired.
   - Slice and serve.

Enjoy your delicious Key Lime Pie!

Coconut Macaroons

Ingredients:

- 2 1/2 cups shredded unsweetened coconut
- 1 cup sweetened condensed milk
- 1/4 cup all-purpose flour
- 1/2 tsp vanilla extract
- 1/4 tsp almond extract (optional)
- 1/4 tsp salt
- 2 large egg whites
- 1/4 tsp cream of tartar
- 1/4 cup granulated sugar

For the Chocolate Drizzle (optional):

- 1/2 cup semi-sweet chocolate chips
- 1 tbsp coconut oil or butter

Instructions:

1. **Prepare the Oven and Baking Sheet:**
   - Preheat your oven to 325°F (163°C).
   - Line a baking sheet with parchment paper or a silicone baking mat.
2. **Make the Coconut Mixture:**
   - In a large bowl, combine shredded coconut, sweetened condensed milk, flour, vanilla extract, almond extract (if using), and salt. Mix until well combined.
3. **Prepare the Meringue:**
   - In a clean, dry mixing bowl, beat the egg whites with an electric mixer on medium speed until foamy.
   - Add the cream of tartar and continue to beat until soft peaks form.
   - Gradually add granulated sugar, 1 tablespoon at a time, beating on high speed until stiff, glossy peaks form.
4. **Combine the Mixtures:**
   - Gently fold the meringue into the coconut mixture until fully combined. Be careful not to deflate the meringue.
5. **Form the Macaroons:**
   - Use a small cookie scoop or tablespoon to drop rounded mounds of the mixture onto the prepared baking sheet. Space them about 1 inch apart.
6. **Bake the Macaroons:**
   - Bake for 15-20 minutes, or until the edges are golden brown and the centers are set.

- Remove from the oven and let the macaroons cool completely on the baking sheet.
7. **Prepare the Chocolate Drizzle (optional):**
    - In a small microwave-safe bowl, melt the semi-sweet chocolate chips and coconut oil or butter in 30-second intervals, stirring after each, until smooth.
    - Drizzle the melted chocolate over the cooled macaroons.
8. **Serve:**
    - Allow the chocolate to set before serving.

Enjoy your sweet and chewy Coconut Macaroons!

Chocolate-Covered Pineapple Bites

Ingredients:

- 1 fresh pineapple, peeled, cored, and cut into bite-sized chunks
- 8 oz semi-sweet chocolate (or dark/milk chocolate, your choice)
- 1 tbsp coconut oil or butter (optional, for smooth melting)
- Crushed nuts, sprinkles, or shredded coconut (optional, for garnish)

Instructions:

1. **Prepare the Pineapple:**
   - Cut the pineapple into bite-sized chunks and place them on a parchment-lined baking sheet. Freeze for at least 30 minutes to firm up.
2. **Melt the Chocolate:**
   - In a heatproof bowl, combine the chocolate and coconut oil or butter (if using).
   - Melt the chocolate using a microwave in 30-second intervals, stirring between each interval until smooth. Alternatively, melt the chocolate over a double boiler on the stovetop.
3. **Dip the Pineapple:**
   - Using a fork or toothpick, dip each frozen pineapple chunk into the melted chocolate, coating it completely.
   - Allow any excess chocolate to drip off before placing the dipped pineapple back onto the parchment-lined baking sheet.
4. **Add Garnishes (optional):**
   - If desired, sprinkle the chocolate-covered pineapple bites with crushed nuts, sprinkles, or shredded coconut before the chocolate sets.
5. **Chill and Serve:**
   - Refrigerate the dipped pineapple bites for about 15-20 minutes, or until the chocolate is set.
   - Serve chilled.

Enjoy your refreshing and indulgent Chocolate-Covered Pineapple Bites!

Jamaican Rum Cake

Ingredients:

For the Cake:

- 1 cup mixed dried fruit (raisins, currants, chopped prunes, etc.)
- 1/2 cup dark rum (for soaking fruit)
- 1 cup all-purpose flour
- 1/2 cup almond flour (or ground almonds)
- 1/2 tsp baking powder
- 1/4 tsp baking soda
- 1/4 tsp salt
- 1/2 cup unsalted butter, softened
- 1 cup granulated sugar
- 4 large eggs
- 1/2 cup molasses
- 1/2 cup fresh orange juice
- 1 tsp vanilla extract
- 1 tsp ground allspice
- 1/2 tsp ground cinnamon
- 1/2 tsp ground nutmeg
- 1/4 tsp ground cloves

For the Glaze (optional):

- 1/4 cup dark rum
- 1/4 cup granulated sugar

Instructions:

1. **Soak the Fruit:**
   - In a bowl, combine the mixed dried fruit and dark rum. Let soak for at least 24 hours, or up to a week for more flavor.
2. **Prepare the Cake Batter:**
   - Preheat your oven to 325°F (163°C). Grease and flour a 9-inch bundt pan or two 8-inch round cake pans.
   - In a medium bowl, whisk together flour, almond flour, baking powder, baking soda, and salt.
   - In a large bowl, cream together the softened butter and granulated sugar until light and fluffy.
   - Beat in the eggs one at a time, then mix in molasses, orange juice, and vanilla extract.

- Gradually add the dry ingredients to the wet ingredients, mixing until just combined.
- Fold in the soaked dried fruit (including any remaining rum) and the spices.
3. **Bake the Cake:**
    - Pour the batter into the prepared pan(s) and smooth the top.
    - Bake for 45-60 minutes, or until a toothpick inserted into the center comes out clean.
    - Allow the cake to cool in the pan for 10 minutes, then transfer to a wire rack to cool completely.
4. **Prepare the Glaze (optional):**
    - In a small saucepan, combine dark rum and granulated sugar.
    - Heat over medium heat, stirring until the sugar is dissolved. Allow to cool slightly.
5. **Glaze the Cake (optional):**
    - Once the cake is completely cool, brush or drizzle the rum glaze over the cake.

Enjoy your flavorful and festive Jamaican Rum Cake!

Mango-Lime Tart

Ingredients:

For the Crust:

- 1 1/2 cups graham cracker crumbs
- 1/4 cup granulated sugar
- 1/2 cup unsalted butter, melted

For the Filling:

- 1 cup fresh mango puree (from about 2 ripe mangoes)
- 1/2 cup sweetened condensed milk
- 1/2 cup fresh lime juice
- 3 large egg yolks
- Zest of 2 limes
- 1/4 cup heavy cream

For the Topping:

- 1 cup heavy cream
- 2 tbsp powdered sugar
- 1/2 tsp vanilla extract
- Lime zest or mango slices for garnish

Instructions:

1. **Prepare the Crust:**
   - Preheat your oven to 350°F (175°C).
   - In a medium bowl, mix graham cracker crumbs, granulated sugar, and melted butter until well combined.
   - Press the mixture evenly into the bottom and up the sides of a 9-inch tart pan.
   - Bake for 8-10 minutes, or until the crust is lightly golden. Remove from the oven and let it cool.
2. **Prepare the Filling:**
   - In a large bowl, whisk together mango puree, sweetened condensed milk, lime juice, egg yolks, and lime zest until smooth and well combined.
   - Pour the filling into the cooled tart crust.
3. **Bake the Tart:**
   - Bake for 15-20 minutes, or until the filling is set and slightly puffed. The center should be firm but still slightly jiggly.
   - Remove from the oven and let it cool to room temperature. Refrigerate for at least 2 hours to fully set.

4. **Prepare the Topping:**
    - In a medium bowl, whip the heavy cream with an electric mixer until soft peaks form.
    - Add powdered sugar and vanilla extract, and continue to whip until stiff peaks form.
5. **Assemble and Serve:**
    - Spread or pipe the whipped cream over the chilled tart.
    - Garnish with additional lime zest or fresh mango slices if desired.
    - Slice and serve.

Enjoy your bright and refreshing Mango-Lime Tart!

Pineapple Coconut Panna Cotta

Ingredients:

For the Panna Cotta:

- 1 cup coconut milk
- 1 cup heavy cream
- 1/2 cup granulated sugar
- 1/2 cup fresh pineapple juice
- 2 tsp gelatin powder
- 3 tbsp water (for blooming gelatin)
- 1 tsp vanilla extract

For the Pineapple Sauce:

- 1 cup fresh pineapple, diced
- 1/4 cup granulated sugar
- 1 tbsp lemon juice

Instructions:

1. **Prepare the Panna Cotta:**
    - In a small bowl, sprinkle the gelatin over 3 tablespoons of cold water. Let it sit for 5 minutes to bloom.
    - In a medium saucepan, combine coconut milk, heavy cream, and granulated sugar. Heat over medium heat until the sugar is dissolved and the mixture is hot but not boiling.
    - Remove the saucepan from heat and stir in the bloomed gelatin until completely dissolved.
    - Stir in the pineapple juice and vanilla extract.
    - Pour the mixture into serving glasses or ramekins. Refrigerate for at least 4 hours, or until set.
2. **Prepare the Pineapple Sauce:**
    - In a small saucepan, combine diced pineapple, granulated sugar, and lemon juice.
    - Cook over medium heat, stirring occasionally, until the pineapple is soft and the sauce has thickened slightly, about 10 minutes.
    - Allow the sauce to cool to room temperature.
3. **Serve:**
    - Once the panna cotta has set, spoon the pineapple sauce over the top of each serving.
    - Garnish with additional pineapple pieces or mint leaves if desired.

Enjoy your creamy and tropical Pineapple Coconut Panna Cotta!

Banana Rum Bread Pudding

Ingredients:

For the Bread Pudding:

- 4 cups cubed stale bread (preferably brioche or challah)
- 2 ripe bananas, mashed
- 2 cups whole milk
- 1 cup heavy cream
- 1/2 cup granulated sugar
- 1/4 cup dark rum
- 3 large eggs
- 1 tsp vanilla extract
- 1 tsp ground cinnamon
- 1/2 tsp ground nutmeg
- 1/4 tsp salt

For the Sauce (optional):

- 1/4 cup butter
- 1/4 cup brown sugar
- 2 tbsp dark rum
- 1/4 cup heavy cream

Instructions:

1. **Prepare the Bread Pudding:**
    - Preheat your oven to 350°F (175°C).
    - Grease a 9x13-inch baking dish.
    - Place the cubed bread in a large mixing bowl. Add the mashed bananas and gently mix.
    - In another bowl, whisk together milk, heavy cream, granulated sugar, dark rum, eggs, vanilla extract, cinnamon, nutmeg, and salt until well combined.
    - Pour the mixture over the bread and bananas, pressing down gently to ensure the bread absorbs the liquid.
    - Let the mixture sit for about 15 minutes, allowing the bread to soak.
2. **Bake the Bread Pudding:**
    - Pour the soaked bread mixture into the prepared baking dish.
    - Bake for 45-50 minutes, or until the pudding is set and the top is golden brown.
3. **Prepare the Sauce (optional):**
    - In a small saucepan, melt the butter over medium heat.
    - Stir in brown sugar and cook until the mixture is smooth and slightly caramelized.
    - Add dark rum and cook for an additional 1-2 minutes.

- - Stir in heavy cream and cook until the sauce is smooth and slightly thickened.
4. **Serve:**
    - Let the bread pudding cool slightly before serving.
    - Drizzle the warm sauce over individual portions of bread pudding or serve on the side.

Enjoy your comforting and flavorful Banana Rum Bread Pudding!

Tropical Fruit Salad with Mint

Ingredients:

- 1 cup fresh pineapple, cut into bite-sized chunks
- 1 cup fresh mango, peeled and diced
- 1 cup fresh papaya, peeled and diced
- 1 cup fresh kiwi, peeled and sliced
- 1 cup strawberries, hulled and halved
- 1/2 cup blueberries
- 1/4 cup fresh mint leaves, chopped
- 1-2 tbsp honey or agave syrup (optional, to taste)
- Juice of 1 lime

Instructions:

1. **Prepare the Fruit:**
   - In a large mixing bowl, combine pineapple, mango, papaya, kiwi, strawberries, and blueberries.
2. **Prepare the Dressing:**
   - In a small bowl, whisk together lime juice and honey or agave syrup (if using). Adjust sweetness to taste.
3. **Combine and Toss:**
   - Pour the dressing over the fruit.
   - Gently toss to coat the fruit evenly with the dressing.
4. **Add Mint:**
   - Sprinkle chopped mint leaves over the fruit salad.
   - Gently toss again to distribute the mint.
5. **Chill and Serve:**
   - Refrigerate the fruit salad for at least 30 minutes before serving to allow flavors to meld.
   - Serve chilled.

Enjoy your vibrant and refreshing Tropical Fruit Salad with Mint!

Coconut Almond Bars

Ingredients:

For the Crust:

- 1 1/2 cups all-purpose flour
- 1/2 cup granulated sugar
- 1/2 cup unsalted butter, softened
- 1/4 cup sliced almonds

For the Filling:

- 1 cup sweetened shredded coconut
- 1/2 cup sliced almonds
- 1/2 cup sweetened condensed milk
- 1/4 cup unsalted butter, melted
- 1/4 tsp salt
- 1/2 tsp vanilla extract

Instructions:

1. **Prepare the Crust:**
    - Preheat your oven to 350°F (175°C).
    - Grease and line an 8x8-inch baking pan with parchment paper.
    - In a medium bowl, mix flour and granulated sugar. Cut in the softened butter until the mixture resembles coarse crumbs.
    - Press the mixture evenly into the bottom of the prepared pan.
    - Sprinkle sliced almonds over the crust.
2. **Bake the Crust:**
    - Bake for 12-15 minutes, or until the crust is lightly golden. Remove from the oven and set aside.
3. **Prepare the Filling:**
    - In a large bowl, combine shredded coconut, sliced almonds, sweetened condensed milk, melted butter, salt, and vanilla extract.
    - Spread the mixture evenly over the partially baked crust.
4. **Bake the Bars:**
    - Return the pan to the oven and bake for an additional 20-25 minutes, or until the top is golden brown and the filling is set.
    - Allow the bars to cool completely in the pan before cutting into squares.

Enjoy your delicious Coconut Almond Bars!

Passion Fruit Mousse

Ingredients:

- 1 cup fresh passion fruit juice (about 6-8 passion fruits)
- 1/2 cup granulated sugar
- 1/4 cup water
- 1 1/2 tsp gelatin powder
- 1 cup heavy cream
- 3 large egg yolks
- 1 tsp vanilla extract

Instructions:

1. **Prepare the Gelatin:**
   - In a small bowl, sprinkle the gelatin over the water. Let it sit for 5 minutes to bloom.
2. **Make the Passion Fruit Mixture:**
   - In a saucepan, combine passion fruit juice and granulated sugar. Heat over medium heat until the sugar dissolves. Remove from heat.
   - Stir in the bloomed gelatin until completely dissolved.
3. **Prepare the Custard:**
   - In a medium bowl, whisk the egg yolks.
   - Gradually whisk in the warm passion fruit mixture to temper the yolks.
   - Return the mixture to the saucepan and cook over medium-low heat, stirring constantly, until it thickens slightly and coats the back of a spoon (about 3-4 minutes). Do not boil.
4. **Cool and Whip:**
   - Remove from heat and stir in vanilla extract.
   - Let the custard cool to room temperature.
   - In a separate bowl, whip the heavy cream until soft peaks form.
   - Gently fold the whipped cream into the cooled passion fruit custard until fully combined.
5. **Chill and Serve:**
   - Spoon the mousse into serving glasses or bowls.
   - Refrigerate for at least 2 hours, or until set.

Enjoy your light and tangy Passion Fruit Mousse!

Papaya and Lime Granita

Ingredients:

- 2 cups fresh papaya, peeled, seeded, and chopped
- 1/2 cup fresh lime juice (about 4 limes)
- 1/2 cup granulated sugar (adjust to taste)
- 1 cup water
- Lime zest (for garnish, optional)

Instructions:

1. **Prepare the Papaya Mixture:**
   - In a blender or food processor, combine the papaya, lime juice, granulated sugar, and water. Blend until smooth.
2. **Chill and Freeze:**
   - Pour the mixture into a shallow baking dish.
   - Freeze for about 1 hour, then stir with a fork to break up any ice crystals.
3. **Scrape and Serve:**
   - Continue to freeze, scraping with a fork every 30 minutes, until the granita is fully frozen and has a fluffy texture (about 3-4 hours total).
4. **Garnish and Serve:**
   - Scoop the granita into serving glasses or bowls.
   - Garnish with lime zest if desired.

Enjoy your refreshing Papaya and Lime Granita!

Banana Foster

Ingredients:

- 4 ripe bananas, peeled and sliced lengthwise or into rounds
- 1/4 cup unsalted butter
- 1/2 cup brown sugar, packed
- 1/4 cup dark rum
- 1/4 cup banana liqueur (optional)
- 1/2 tsp ground cinnamon
- 1/4 tsp ground nutmeg
- Vanilla ice cream (for serving)

Instructions:

1. **Prepare the Sauce:**
   - In a large skillet, melt the butter over medium heat.
   - Stir in the brown sugar, cinnamon, and nutmeg. Cook, stirring occasionally, until the sugar is dissolved and the mixture is bubbling (about 2-3 minutes).
2. **Cook the Bananas:**
   - Add the sliced bananas to the skillet. Cook for 1-2 minutes on each side, or until the bananas are tender and coated with the sauce.
3. **Add the Alcohol:**
   - Carefully pour in the dark rum and banana liqueur (if using). Allow the mixture to simmer for about 1 minute.
   - If you're comfortable with flambéing, carefully ignite the alcohol with a long lighter to burn off the alcohol, then let it burn out on its own. If not, just allow it to simmer for an extra minute to let the alcohol cook off.
4. **Serve:**
   - Spoon the bananas and sauce over scoops of vanilla ice cream.

Enjoy your rich and delicious Banana Foster!

Coconut Cream Pie

Ingredients:

For the Pie Crust:

- 1 1/2 cups graham cracker crumbs
- 1/4 cup granulated sugar
- 1/2 cup unsalted butter, melted

For the Filling:

- 1 can (13.5 oz) coconut milk
- 1 cup whole milk
- 3/4 cup granulated sugar
- 1/4 cup cornstarch
- 1/4 tsp salt
- 4 large egg yolks
- 1/2 cup shredded sweetened coconut
- 1 tsp vanilla extract

For the Topping:

- 1 cup heavy cream
- 2 tbsp powdered sugar
- 1/2 tsp vanilla extract
- Shredded coconut, toasted (for garnish)

Instructions:

1. **Prepare the Pie Crust:**
    - Preheat your oven to 350°F (175°C).
    - In a medium bowl, combine graham cracker crumbs, granulated sugar, and melted butter. Mix until well combined.
    - Press the mixture evenly into the bottom and up the sides of a 9-inch pie pan.
    - Bake for 8-10 minutes, or until the crust is lightly golden. Remove from the oven and let it cool completely.
2. **Prepare the Filling:**
    - In a medium saucepan, combine coconut milk, whole milk, granulated sugar, cornstarch, and salt. Whisk to combine.
    - Heat the mixture over medium heat, whisking constantly, until it begins to thicken and comes to a gentle boil.
    - Remove from heat and whisk in egg yolks one at a time, then return to heat. Cook, stirring constantly, until the mixture thickens further (about 1-2 minutes).

    - Stir in shredded coconut and vanilla extract.
    - Pour the filling into the cooled pie crust and smooth the top with a spatula.
3. **Chill the Pie:**
    - Refrigerate the pie for at least 4 hours, or until fully set.
4. **Prepare the Topping:**
    - In a medium bowl, whip the heavy cream with an electric mixer until soft peaks form.
    - Add powdered sugar and vanilla extract, and continue to whip until stiff peaks form.
5. **Assemble and Serve:**
    - Spread or pipe the whipped cream over the chilled pie.
    - Garnish with toasted shredded coconut.

Enjoy your creamy and delicious Coconut Cream Pie!

Pineapple Coconut Cupcakes

Ingredients:

For the Cupcakes:

- 1 1/2 cups all-purpose flour
- 1 cup granulated sugar
- 1/2 cup unsweetened shredded coconut
- 1 1/2 tsp baking powder
- 1/2 tsp baking soda
- 1/4 tsp salt
- 1/2 cup unsalted butter, softened
- 2 large eggs
- 1/2 cup crushed pineapple, drained
- 1/2 cup sour cream
- 1/4 cup coconut milk
- 1 tsp vanilla extract

For the Coconut Frosting:

- 1/2 cup unsalted butter, softened
- 2 cups powdered sugar
- 2 tbsp coconut milk
- 1/2 tsp vanilla extract
- 1/2 cup unsweetened shredded coconut (for garnish)

Instructions:

1. **Prepare the Cupcakes:**
    - Preheat your oven to 350°F (175°C). Line a 12-cup muffin pan with paper liners.
    - In a medium bowl, whisk together flour, sugar, shredded coconut, baking powder, baking soda, and salt.
    - In a large bowl, cream together the softened butter and granulated sugar until light and fluffy.
    - Beat in the eggs one at a time, mixing well after each addition.
    - Mix in the crushed pineapple, sour cream, coconut milk, and vanilla extract.
    - Gradually add the dry ingredients to the wet ingredients, mixing until just combined.
2. **Bake the Cupcakes:**
    - Divide the batter evenly among the 12 muffin cups, filling each about 2/3 full.
    - Bake for 18-22 minutes, or until a toothpick inserted into the center comes out clean.

- Allow the cupcakes to cool in the pan for 5 minutes before transferring them to a wire rack to cool completely.
3. **Prepare the Coconut Frosting:**
    - In a medium bowl, beat the softened butter with an electric mixer until creamy.
    - Gradually add the powdered sugar, beating until smooth.
    - Mix in coconut milk and vanilla extract until the frosting is light and fluffy.
4. **Frost the Cupcakes:**
    - Once the cupcakes are completely cool, frost with the coconut frosting using a spatula or piping bag.
    - Sprinkle the top of each cupcake with shredded coconut.

Enjoy your delightful Pineapple Coconut Cupcakes!

Guava Sorbet

Ingredients:

- 2 cups fresh guava juice (from about 6-8 ripe guavas) or canned guava juice
- 1 cup granulated sugar
- 1/2 cup water
- 1 tablespoon lime juice (optional, for added tartness)
- 1 tablespoon lime zest (optional, for added flavor)

Instructions:

1. **Prepare the Simple Syrup:**
    - In a small saucepan, combine the granulated sugar and water.
    - Heat over medium heat, stirring constantly, until the sugar is completely dissolved.
    - Remove from heat and let it cool to room temperature.
2. **Combine Ingredients:**
    - In a large bowl, mix the guava juice with the cooled simple syrup.
    - Add lime juice and lime zest if using. Stir well to combine.
3. **Chill the Mixture:**
    - Refrigerate the mixture for at least 1 hour to chill.
4. **Freeze the Sorbet:**
    - Pour the chilled mixture into an ice cream maker and churn according to the manufacturer's instructions, usually for about 20-25 minutes, until it reaches a sorbet-like consistency.
    - If you don't have an ice cream maker, pour the mixture into a shallow dish and freeze. Every 30 minutes, stir the mixture with a fork to break up ice crystals until it is fully frozen (about 3-4 hours).
5. **Serve:**
    - Scoop the sorbet into serving bowls or glasses.
    - Garnish with fresh mint leaves or a slice of guava, if desired.

Enjoy your refreshing and tropical Guava Sorbet!

Tropical Tiramisu

Ingredients:

For the Filling:

- 8 oz (225 g) mascarpone cheese, softened
- 1 cup heavy cream
- 1/2 cup granulated sugar
- 1 tsp vanilla extract
- 1/2 cup coconut milk
- 1/2 cup crushed pineapple, drained
- 1/2 cup diced mango
- 1/4 cup rum or coconut liqueur (optional)

For the Layers:

- 24 ladyfingers (savoiardi)
- 1 cup pineapple juice or coconut milk (for soaking)

For Garnish:

- Shredded coconut, toasted
- Fresh fruit (mango slices, pineapple chunks, etc.)

Instructions:

1. **Prepare the Filling:**
    - In a large bowl, beat the mascarpone cheese with an electric mixer until smooth.
    - In another bowl, whip the heavy cream until soft peaks form.
    - Gently fold the whipped cream into the mascarpone cheese.
    - Stir in the granulated sugar, vanilla extract, coconut milk, and crushed pineapple. Mix until well combined.
2. **Prepare the Ladyfingers:**
    - Lightly soak each ladyfinger in pineapple juice or coconut milk for about 2 seconds (do not soak too long as they can become soggy).
3. **Assemble the Tiramisu:**
    - In a 9x9-inch or similar-sized dish, arrange a layer of soaked ladyfingers on the bottom.
    - Spread half of the mascarpone mixture over the ladyfingers.
    - Add a layer of diced mango.
    - Repeat with another layer of soaked ladyfingers and the remaining mascarpone mixture.
    - Drizzle with rum or coconut liqueur, if using.

4. **Chill and Serve:**
    - Cover and refrigerate the tiramisu for at least 4 hours, or overnight, to allow flavors to meld and the dessert to set.
    - Before serving, garnish with toasted shredded coconut and fresh fruit.

Enjoy your tropical twist on classic tiramisu!

Mango Chia Seed Pudding

Ingredients:

- 1 cup coconut milk (or any plant-based milk)
- 1/2 cup mango puree (fresh or canned)
- 1/4 cup chia seeds
- 2-3 tbsp maple syrup or honey (to taste)
- 1/2 tsp vanilla extract (optional)
- Fresh mango slices (for garnish)
- Shredded coconut (for garnish, optional)

Instructions:

1. **Combine Ingredients:**
   - In a medium bowl, whisk together coconut milk, mango puree, chia seeds, maple syrup or honey, and vanilla extract if using.
2. **Chill:**
   - Cover the bowl and refrigerate for at least 4 hours, or overnight. Stir occasionally to prevent the chia seeds from clumping.
3. **Serve:**
   - Once the pudding has thickened and the chia seeds have expanded, give it a good stir.
   - Spoon into serving glasses or bowls.
4. **Garnish:**
   - Top with fresh mango slices and a sprinkle of shredded coconut, if desired.

Enjoy your refreshing Mango Chia Seed Pudding!

Pineapple Upside-Down Cupcakes

Ingredients:

For the Topping:

- 1/4 cup unsalted butter
- 1/2 cup brown sugar, packed
- 1/2 cup crushed pineapple, drained
- Maraschino cherries (optional, for garnish)

For the Cupcake Batter:

- 1 1/2 cups all-purpose flour
- 1 cup granulated sugar
- 1 1/2 tsp baking powder
- 1/2 tsp baking soda
- 1/4 tsp salt
- 1/2 cup unsalted butter, softened
- 2 large eggs
- 1/2 cup sour cream
- 1/2 cup pineapple juice
- 1 tsp vanilla extract

Instructions:

1. **Prepare the Topping:**
    - Preheat your oven to 350°F (175°C). Line a 12-cup muffin pan with paper liners.
    - In a small saucepan, melt the butter over medium heat. Stir in the brown sugar and cook until the mixture is smooth and bubbly (about 2-3 minutes). Remove from heat.
    - Spoon a small amount of the brown sugar mixture into the bottom of each cupcake liner.
    - Place a spoonful of crushed pineapple on top of the brown sugar mixture in each liner. If using, place a maraschino cherry in the center of the pineapple.
2. **Prepare the Cupcake Batter:**
    - In a medium bowl, whisk together flour, granulated sugar, baking powder, baking soda, and salt.
    - In a large bowl, cream together the softened butter and sugar until light and fluffy.
    - Beat in the eggs one at a time, mixing well after each addition.
    - Mix in the sour cream, pineapple juice, and vanilla extract until smooth.
    - Gradually add the dry ingredients to the wet ingredients, mixing until just combined.
3. **Assemble and Bake:**

- Spoon the cupcake batter evenly over the pineapple topping in each liner, filling about 2/3 full.
- Bake for 18-22 minutes, or until a toothpick inserted into the center comes out clean.
- Allow the cupcakes to cool in the pan for 5 minutes before transferring them to a wire rack to cool completely.

4. **Serve:**
   - Once completely cooled, carefully remove the paper liners to reveal the pineapple topping.

Enjoy your delicious Pineapple Upside-Down Cupcakes!

Coconut Pineapple Bread

Ingredients:

- 1 1/2 cups all-purpose flour
- 1 cup granulated sugar
- 1 tsp baking powder
- 1/2 tsp baking soda
- 1/4 tsp salt
- 1/2 cup unsalted butter, softened
- 1/2 cup crushed pineapple, drained
- 1/2 cup shredded coconut
- 2 large eggs
- 1/2 cup sour cream or Greek yogurt
- 1/4 cup coconut milk
- 1 tsp vanilla extract

Instructions:

1. **Prepare the Oven and Pan:**
    - Preheat your oven to 350°F (175°C).
    - Grease and flour a 9x5-inch loaf pan.
2. **Mix Dry Ingredients:**
    - In a medium bowl, whisk together flour, sugar, baking powder, baking soda, and salt.
3. **Mix Wet Ingredients:**
    - In a large bowl, cream the softened butter until light and fluffy.
    - Beat in the eggs one at a time.
    - Add the sour cream, coconut milk, and vanilla extract. Mix until smooth.
4. **Combine Ingredients:**
    - Gradually add the dry ingredients to the wet ingredients, mixing until just combined.
    - Fold in the crushed pineapple and shredded coconut.
5. **Bake:**
    - Pour the batter into the prepared loaf pan.
    - Bake for 50-60 minutes, or until a toothpick inserted into the center comes out clean.
    - Let the bread cool in the pan for 10 minutes before transferring to a wire rack to cool completely.

Enjoy your moist and flavorful Coconut Pineapple Bread!

Rum and Raisin Rice Pudding

Ingredients:

- 1/2 cup short-grain or arborio rice
- 2 cups whole milk
- 1 cup heavy cream
- 1/2 cup granulated sugar
- 1/2 cup raisins
- 2 tbsp dark rum
- 1/2 tsp vanilla extract
- 1/2 tsp ground cinnamon (optional, for added flavor)
- A pinch of salt

Instructions:

1. **Prepare the Rice:**
    - In a medium saucepan, combine rice, milk, and a pinch of salt. Bring to a gentle boil over medium heat.
2. **Cook the Rice:**
    - Reduce heat to low and simmer, stirring occasionally, until the rice is tender and the mixture has thickened (about 20-25 minutes).
3. **Add Raisins and Flavorings:**
    - Stir in the sugar, raisins, and ground cinnamon (if using). Continue to cook for an additional 5 minutes, or until the raisins are plumped and the pudding has thickened to your desired consistency.
4. **Finish the Pudding:**
    - Remove from heat and stir in the vanilla extract and dark rum.
5. **Cool and Serve:**
    - Allow the pudding to cool slightly before serving. It can be served warm or chilled.
    - Spoon into serving bowls and garnish with a sprinkle of cinnamon or additional raisins if desired.

Enjoy your rich and creamy Rum and Raisin Rice Pudding!

Spiced Apple and Coconut Crumble

Ingredients:

For the Filling:

- 6 cups apples, peeled, cored, and sliced (about 4-5 medium apples)
- 1/4 cup granulated sugar
- 1/4 cup brown sugar
- 1 tsp ground cinnamon
- 1/4 tsp ground nutmeg
- 1 tbsp lemon juice
- 2 tbsp all-purpose flour

For the Crumble Topping:

- 1 cup all-purpose flour
- 1/2 cup rolled oats
- 1/2 cup shredded coconut
- 1/2 cup brown sugar
- 1/2 cup unsalted butter, cold and cut into small pieces
- 1/4 tsp ground cinnamon
- A pinch of salt

Instructions:

1. **Prepare the Filling:**
   - Preheat your oven to 350°F (175°C).
   - In a large bowl, toss the sliced apples with granulated sugar, brown sugar, ground cinnamon, nutmeg, lemon juice, and flour until well coated.
   - Transfer the apple mixture to a 9x9-inch baking dish or similar-sized ovenproof dish.
2. **Prepare the Crumble Topping:**
   - In a separate bowl, combine flour, rolled oats, shredded coconut, brown sugar, ground cinnamon, and a pinch of salt.
   - Cut in the cold butter using a pastry cutter or your fingers until the mixture resembles coarse crumbs.
3. **Assemble and Bake:**
   - Sprinkle the crumble topping evenly over the apple mixture.
   - Bake for 35-45 minutes, or until the topping is golden brown and the apple filling is bubbling.
4. **Serve:**
   - Allow the crumble to cool slightly before serving.

Enjoy your comforting Spiced Apple and Coconut Crumble!

Passion Fruit Jelly

Ingredients:

- 1 cup fresh passion fruit juice (from about 6-8 passion fruits) or store-bought
- 1/2 cup granulated sugar (adjust to taste)
- 1/4 cup water
- 1 tablespoon lemon juice
- 1 tablespoon powdered gelatin (or 1 packet, usually 1/4 ounce)
- Fresh passion fruit seeds or mint leaves (for garnish, optional)

Instructions:

1. **Prepare the Gelatin:**
   - In a small bowl, sprinkle the powdered gelatin over 1/4 cup water. Let it sit for about 5 minutes to bloom.
2. **Heat the Juice Mixture:**
   - In a saucepan, combine the passion fruit juice, granulated sugar, and lemon juice.
   - Heat over medium heat, stirring occasionally, until the sugar is dissolved and the mixture is hot (but not boiling).
3. **Dissolve the Gelatin:**
   - Remove the saucepan from heat.
   - Stir the bloomed gelatin into the hot passion fruit mixture until fully dissolved.
4. **Chill the Jelly:**
   - Pour the mixture into jelly molds or individual serving glasses.
   - Allow it to cool to room temperature.
   - Refrigerate for at least 4 hours, or until set.
5. **Serve:**
   - Once set, garnish with fresh passion fruit seeds or mint leaves, if desired.

Enjoy your vibrant and refreshing Passion Fruit Jelly!

Tropical Fruit Tartlets

Ingredients:

For the Tartlet Shells:

- 1 1/2 cups all-purpose flour
- 1/4 cup granulated sugar
- 1/2 cup unsalted butter, cold and cubed
- 1 large egg yolk
- 2-3 tbsp cold water

For the Filling:

- 1 cup pastry cream (store-bought or homemade)
- 1/2 cup diced tropical fruits (such as mango, pineapple, and kiwi)

For Garnish:

- Fresh mint leaves
- Shredded coconut (optional)

Instructions:

1. **Prepare the Tartlet Shells:**
   - Preheat your oven to 375°F (190°C).
   - In a food processor, combine flour and granulated sugar. Add the cold butter and pulse until the mixture resembles coarse crumbs.
   - Add the egg yolk and pulse until just combined. Gradually add cold water, 1 tablespoon at a time, until the dough comes together.
   - Roll out the dough on a lightly floured surface and cut into circles to fit into your tartlet pans.
   - Press the dough into the tartlet pans and trim the edges. Prick the bottoms with a fork to prevent bubbling.
   - Bake for 12-15 minutes, or until the tartlet shells are golden brown. Let them cool completely.
2. **Prepare the Filling:**
   - Spoon or pipe the pastry cream into the cooled tartlet shells.
   - Top with diced tropical fruits.
3. **Garnish and Serve:**
   - Garnish with fresh mint leaves and a sprinkle of shredded coconut, if desired.

Enjoy your delightful Tropical Fruit Tartlets!

Key Lime Bars

Ingredients:

For the Crust:

- 1 1/2 cups graham cracker crumbs
- 1/4 cup granulated sugar
- 1/2 cup unsalted butter, melted

For the Filling:

- 1 can (14 oz) sweetened condensed milk
- 1/2 cup fresh key lime juice (about 8-10 key limes)
- 3 large egg yolks
- 1/2 tsp vanilla extract

For the Topping:

- 1/2 cup heavy cream
- 2 tbsp powdered sugar
- Lime zest (for garnish)

Instructions:

1. **Prepare the Crust:**
    - Preheat your oven to 350°F (175°C).
    - In a medium bowl, combine graham cracker crumbs, granulated sugar, and melted butter. Mix until well combined.
    - Press the mixture evenly into the bottom of an 8x8-inch baking dish lined with parchment paper.
2. **Bake the Crust:**
    - Bake for 8-10 minutes, or until the crust is lightly golden. Let it cool.
3. **Prepare the Filling:**
    - In a large bowl, whisk together sweetened condensed milk, key lime juice, egg yolks, and vanilla extract until smooth.
    - Pour the filling over the cooled crust.
4. **Bake the Bars:**
    - Bake for 15-20 minutes, or until the filling is set and the edges are slightly firm.
    - Allow the bars to cool completely before refrigerating for at least 2 hours to fully set.
5. **Prepare the Topping:**
    - In a medium bowl, whip the heavy cream with powdered sugar until soft peaks form.
6. **Serve:**
    - Spread or pipe the whipped cream over the chilled bars.
    - Garnish with lime zest before cutting into squares.

Enjoy your tangy and refreshing Key Lime Bars!

Coconut Banana Smoothie Bowl

Ingredients:

- 2 ripe bananas, sliced and frozen
- 1/2 cup coconut milk (or any plant-based milk)
- 1/4 cup Greek yogurt (optional, for added creaminess)
- 1 tbsp honey or maple syrup (optional, for sweetness)
- 1/2 tsp vanilla extract (optional)

For Toppings:

- Sliced fresh bananas
- Shredded coconut
- Granola
- Fresh berries (e.g., strawberries, blueberries)
- Chia seeds or flaxseeds

Instructions:

1. **Blend the Smoothie:**
    - In a blender, combine the frozen bananas, coconut milk, Greek yogurt (if using), honey or maple syrup, and vanilla extract.
    - Blend until smooth and creamy, adding more coconut milk if needed to reach your desired consistency.
2. **Serve:**
    - Pour the smoothie into a bowl.
    - Top with sliced fresh bananas, shredded coconut, granola, fresh berries, and chia seeds or flaxseeds.

Enjoy your delicious and nutritious Coconut Banana Smoothie Bowl!

Pineapple Coconut Rice Pudding

Ingredients:

- 1/2 cup short-grain or arborio rice
- 1 cup coconut milk
- 1 cup whole milk
- 1/2 cup granulated sugar
- 1/2 cup crushed pineapple, drained
- 1/4 cup shredded coconut
- 1/2 tsp vanilla extract
- A pinch of salt

Instructions:

1. **Cook the Rice:**
    - In a medium saucepan, combine rice, coconut milk, whole milk, and a pinch of salt. Bring to a gentle boil over medium heat.
2. **Simmer:**
    - Reduce heat to low and simmer, stirring occasionally, until the rice is tender and the mixture has thickened (about 20-25 minutes).
3. **Add Ingredients:**
    - Stir in the sugar, crushed pineapple, and shredded coconut. Cook for an additional 5 minutes, or until well combined and thickened.
4. **Finish and Serve:**
    - Remove from heat and stir in vanilla extract.
    - Spoon into serving dishes and allow to cool slightly before serving.

Enjoy your creamy Pineapple Coconut Rice Pudding!

Mango and Coconut Ice Cream

Ingredients:

- 2 cups ripe mangoes, peeled and diced (about 2-3 mangoes)
- 1 can (13.5 oz) coconut milk
- 1 cup heavy cream
- 1/2 cup granulated sugar (adjust to taste)
- 1 tsp vanilla extract
- Juice of 1 lime (optional, for added tanginess)

Instructions:

1. **Prepare the Mango Puree:**
    - In a blender, combine the diced mangoes and blend until smooth. You should have about 1 1/2 to 2 cups of mango puree.
2. **Combine Ingredients:**
    - In a large bowl, whisk together the mango puree, coconut milk, heavy cream, granulated sugar, and vanilla extract until the sugar is fully dissolved and the mixture is smooth.
    - If using lime juice, stir it in now to add a hint of tartness.
3. **Chill the Mixture:**
    - Refrigerate the mixture for at least 1 hour to chill. This helps the ice cream churn better.
4. **Churn the Ice Cream:**
    - Pour the chilled mixture into an ice cream maker and churn according to the manufacturer's instructions, usually for about 20-25 minutes, until it reaches a soft-serve consistency.
5. **Freeze:**
    - Transfer the churned ice cream to an airtight container and freeze for at least 2 hours to firm up.
6. **Serve:**
    - Scoop the ice cream into bowls or cones and enjoy!

Enjoy your tropical Mango and Coconut Ice Cream!

Pineapple Rum Flan

Ingredients:

For the Caramel:

- 1 cup granulated sugar
- 1/4 cup water

For the Flan:

- 1 can (14 oz) sweetened condensed milk
- 1 can (12 oz) evaporated milk
- 4 large eggs
- 1 cup fresh pineapple juice (or canned)
- 1/4 cup dark rum
- 1 tsp vanilla extract
- 1/4 tsp salt

Instructions:

1. **Prepare the Caramel:**
   - In a medium saucepan over medium heat, combine the granulated sugar and water.
   - Cook, stirring occasionally, until the sugar dissolves and turns a golden amber color. This usually takes about 8-10 minutes.
   - Carefully pour the caramel into the bottom of a 9-inch round cake pan or individual ramekins, tilting the pan to evenly coat the bottom. Set aside to cool and harden.
2. **Prepare the Flan Mixture:**
   - Preheat your oven to 350°F (175°C).
   - In a large bowl, whisk together the sweetened condensed milk, evaporated milk, eggs, pineapple juice, dark rum, vanilla extract, and salt until smooth and well combined.
3. **Pour the Flan Mixture:**
   - Gently pour the flan mixture over the set caramel in the pan(s).
4. **Bake:**
   - Place the pan(s) in a large baking dish. Carefully pour hot water into the baking dish to create a water bath that reaches halfway up the sides of the flan pan(s).
   - Bake for 50-60 minutes, or until the flan is set and a knife inserted into the center comes out clean.
5. **Cool and Unmold:**
   - Remove the flan from the oven and let it cool to room temperature.
   - Refrigerate for at least 4 hours, or overnight, to chill and firm up.

- To unmold, run a knife around the edges of the flan, place a serving plate over the pan, and invert to release the flan.

Enjoy your tropical Pineapple Rum Flan!

Coconut Chocolate Truffles

Ingredients:

- 1 cup semi-sweet chocolate chips or finely chopped chocolate
- 1/2 cup canned coconut milk (full-fat)
- 1/2 cup shredded coconut (for rolling)
- 1/4 cup unsweetened cocoa powder (for rolling, optional)
- 1/2 tsp vanilla extract

Instructions:

1. **Prepare the Ganache:**
    - In a heatproof bowl, combine the chocolate chips and vanilla extract.
    - In a small saucepan, heat the coconut milk over medium heat until it just begins to simmer (do not let it boil).
    - Pour the hot coconut milk over the chocolate and let it sit for 1-2 minutes. Stir until smooth and fully combined.
2. **Chill the Ganache:**
    - Cover the bowl and refrigerate for about 1-2 hours, or until the ganache is firm enough to scoop.
3. **Form the Truffles:**
    - Using a small cookie scoop or your hands, form the ganache into small balls (about 1-inch in diameter).
    - Roll the balls in shredded coconut or cocoa powder to coat.
4. **Chill and Serve:**
    - Place the coated truffles on a parchment-lined tray and refrigerate until firm.

Enjoy your rich and creamy Coconut Chocolate Truffles!

Mango and Pineapple Pavlova

Ingredients:

For the Meringue Base:

- 4 large egg whites
- 1 cup granulated sugar
- 1 tsp cornstarch
- 1/2 tsp white vinegar
- 1/2 tsp vanilla extract

For the Topping:

- 1 cup heavy cream
- 2 tbsp powdered sugar
- 1/2 tsp vanilla extract
- 1 cup fresh mango, peeled and diced
- 1 cup fresh pineapple, peeled and diced
- Fresh mint leaves (for garnish, optional)

Instructions:

1. **Prepare the Meringue Base:**
    - Preheat your oven to 275°F (135°C). Line a baking sheet with parchment paper.
    - In a large, clean mixing bowl, beat the egg whites with an electric mixer until soft peaks form.
    - Gradually add the granulated sugar, beating until stiff, glossy peaks form.
    - Gently fold in the cornstarch, vinegar, and vanilla extract until well combined.
2. **Shape and Bake the Meringue:**
    - Spoon the meringue mixture onto the prepared baking sheet, forming a large circle or oval shape (about 8-10 inches in diameter) with a slight well in the center to hold the toppings.
    - Use a spatula to smooth the edges and create a slight peak in the center.
    - Bake for 1 hour to 1 hour 15 minutes, or until the meringue is crisp and dry on the outside but still soft and marshmallow-like inside.
    - Turn off the oven and let the meringue cool completely in the oven with the door slightly ajar.
3. **Prepare the Whipped Cream:**
    - In a medium bowl, whip the heavy cream with powdered sugar and vanilla extract until soft peaks form.
4. **Assemble the Pavlova:**
    - Once the meringue is completely cool, transfer it to a serving plate.
    - Spread the whipped cream over the top of the meringue.
    - Arrange the diced mango and pineapple on top of the whipped cream.
5. **Garnish and Serve:**
    - Garnish with fresh mint leaves if desired.

- Serve immediately or refrigerate until ready to serve.

Enjoy your tropical Mango and Pineapple Pavlova!

Tropical Fruit Sorbet

Ingredients:

- 2 cups fresh or frozen tropical fruit (e.g., mango, pineapple, or papaya)
- 1/2 cup granulated sugar (adjust to taste)
- 1/2 cup water
- Juice of 1 lime or lemon
- 1/4 cup coconut milk (optional, for added creaminess)

Instructions:

1. **Prepare the Fruit:**
   - If using fresh fruit, peel, core, and chop it into small pieces. If using frozen fruit, make sure it's fully frozen.
2. **Blend the Mixture:**
   - In a blender, combine the fruit, sugar, water, and lime or lemon juice.
   - Blend until smooth. If using coconut milk, blend it in for added creaminess.
3. **Chill the Mixture:**
   - Taste the mixture and adjust the sweetness or acidity if needed. Transfer it to a bowl and refrigerate for about 1 hour to chill.
4. **Churn the Sorbet:**
   - Pour the chilled mixture into an ice cream maker and churn according to the manufacturer's instructions, usually about 20-25 minutes, until it reaches a soft-serve consistency.
5. **Freeze:**
   - Transfer the sorbet to an airtight container and freeze for at least 2 hours to firm up.
6. **Serve:**
   - Scoop into bowls or cones and enjoy!

Enjoy your refreshing Tropical Fruit Sorbet!

Rum-Soaked Coconut Cake

Ingredients:

For the Cake:

- 1 1/2 cups all-purpose flour
- 1 1/2 tsp baking powder
- 1/2 tsp baking soda
- 1/4 tsp salt
- 1/2 cup unsalted butter, softened
- 1 cup granulated sugar
- 2 large eggs
- 1 cup coconut milk
- 1/2 cup shredded coconut
- 1 tsp vanilla extract

For the Rum Soak:

- 1/4 cup dark rum
- 1/4 cup granulated sugar
- 1/4 cup water

For the Frosting (optional):

- 1 cup heavy cream
- 2 tbsp powdered sugar
- 1/2 tsp vanilla extract
- Extra shredded coconut for garnish

Instructions:

1. **Prepare the Cake:**
    - Preheat your oven to 350°F (175°C). Grease and flour an 8-inch round cake pan or a similar-sized baking dish.
    - In a medium bowl, whisk together the flour, baking powder, baking soda, and salt.
    - In a large bowl, cream the softened butter and granulated sugar until light and fluffy.
    - Beat in the eggs, one at a time, then add the vanilla extract.
    - Gradually add the dry ingredients to the wet mixture, alternating with the coconut milk, beginning and ending with the dry ingredients. Mix until just combined.
    - Fold in the shredded coconut.
2. **Bake the Cake:**
    - Pour the batter into the prepared pan and smooth the top.

- Bake for 25-30 minutes, or until a toothpick inserted into the center comes out clean.
- Allow the cake to cool in the pan for 10 minutes before transferring to a wire rack to cool completely.

3. **Prepare the Rum Soak:**
   - In a small saucepan, combine the dark rum, granulated sugar, and water. Heat over medium heat, stirring until the sugar is fully dissolved. Remove from heat and let it cool slightly.

4. **Soak the Cake:**
   - Once the cake is completely cooled, use a fork or skewer to poke holes all over the top.
   - Slowly drizzle the rum soak evenly over the cake, allowing it to absorb.

5. **Prepare the Frosting (optional):**
   - In a medium bowl, whip the heavy cream with powdered sugar and vanilla extract until soft peaks form.
   - Spread or pipe the whipped cream over the soaked cake.
   - Garnish with extra shredded coconut if desired.

Serve and Enjoy:

- Slice and enjoy your moist and flavorful Rum-Soaked Coconut Cake!

This cake combines the rich flavors of coconut and rum, with a hint of sweetness and creaminess if you choose to add the frosting.

Guava Cream Cheese Muffins

Ingredients:

For the Muffins:

- 2 cups all-purpose flour
- 1/2 cup granulated sugar
- 1/4 cup brown sugar, packed
- 1 tbsp baking powder
- 1/2 tsp baking soda
- 1/2 tsp salt
- 1/2 cup unsalted butter, melted
- 2 large eggs
- 1 cup milk
- 1 tsp vanilla extract
- 1 cup guava paste, diced (or guava jam/preserves)
- 1/2 cup shredded coconut (optional)

For the Cream Cheese Filling:

- 4 oz cream cheese, softened
- 1/4 cup granulated sugar
- 1/2 tsp vanilla extract

For the Topping (optional):

- 2 tbsp granulated sugar
- 1/4 tsp ground cinnamon

Instructions:

1. **Prepare the Cream Cheese Filling:**
   - In a small bowl, mix together the softened cream cheese, granulated sugar, and vanilla extract until smooth and well combined. Set aside.
2. **Prepare the Muffins:**
   - Preheat your oven to 375°F (190°C). Line a muffin tin with paper liners or grease it lightly.
   - In a large bowl, whisk together the flour, granulated sugar, brown sugar, baking powder, baking soda, and salt.
   - In another bowl, mix together the melted butter, eggs, milk, and vanilla extract until well combined.
   - Pour the wet ingredients into the dry ingredients and stir until just combined. Do not overmix.
   - Gently fold in the diced guava paste (or guava jam/preserves) and shredded coconut, if using.
3. **Assemble the Muffins:**

- Spoon a small amount of muffin batter into each muffin cup, filling each about 1/3 full.
- Place a small dollop of the cream cheese filling in the center of each muffin.
- Top with additional muffin batter, covering the cream cheese filling completely.

4. **Add Topping (Optional):**
   - If using, mix the granulated sugar and ground cinnamon together and sprinkle a little over the top of each muffin.

5. **Bake:**
   - Bake for 20-25 minutes, or until the muffins are golden brown and a toothpick inserted into the center comes out clean.

6. **Cool:**
   - Allow the muffins to cool in the tin for a few minutes, then transfer to a wire rack to cool completely.

Serve and Enjoy:

- Enjoy your Guava Cream Cheese Muffins warm or at room temperature!

These muffins are perfect for breakfast or a sweet snack, with a delightful combination of creamy cheese and tropical guava flavor.

Pineapple and Coconut Cheesecake Bars

Ingredients:

For the Crust:

- 1 1/2 cups graham cracker crumbs
- 1/4 cup granulated sugar
- 1/2 cup unsalted butter, melted

For the Cheesecake Filling:

- 16 oz (2 packages) cream cheese, softened
- 1 cup granulated sugar
- 3 large eggs
- 1 cup sour cream
- 1 cup canned crushed pineapple, drained
- 1/2 cup shredded coconut
- 1 tsp vanilla extract

For the Topping:

- 1/2 cup shredded coconut, toasted (for garnish)
- Optional: extra crushed pineapple for garnish

Instructions:

1. **Prepare the Crust:**
   - Preheat your oven to 325°F (160°C). Line an 8x8-inch baking pan with parchment paper, leaving some overhang for easy removal.
   - In a medium bowl, combine the graham cracker crumbs, granulated sugar, and melted butter. Mix until the crumbs are evenly coated and resemble wet sand.
   - Press the mixture firmly into the bottom of the prepared baking pan to form an even layer.
   - Bake the crust for 10 minutes, then remove from the oven and let it cool slightly.
2. **Prepare the Cheesecake Filling:**
   - In a large bowl, beat the softened cream cheese and granulated sugar together until smooth and creamy.
   - Add the eggs, one at a time, beating well after each addition.
   - Mix in the sour cream, crushed pineapple, shredded coconut, and vanilla extract until fully combined.
   - Pour the cheesecake filling over the pre-baked crust and smooth the top with a spatula.
3. **Bake:**

- Bake for 40-45 minutes, or until the center is set and the edges are lightly golden. The center should slightly jiggle but not be liquid.
- Turn off the oven and let the cheesecake bars cool in the oven with the door slightly ajar for 1 hour.
4. **Chill:**
    - After cooling, refrigerate the cheesecake bars for at least 4 hours or overnight to fully set.
5. **Prepare the Topping:**
    - Toast the shredded coconut in a dry skillet over medium heat until golden brown, stirring frequently. Be careful not to burn it.
6. **Serve:**
    - Once the cheesecake bars are fully chilled, lift them out of the pan using the parchment paper overhang. Cut into squares.
    - Garnish with toasted shredded coconut and extra crushed pineapple if desired.

Enjoy:

- Enjoy your Pineapple and Coconut Cheesecake Bars chilled!

These bars offer a delightful blend of creamy cheesecake with tropical pineapple and coconut flavors, perfect for a refreshing dessert.

Banana Coconut Muffins

Ingredients:

For the Muffins:

- 1 1/2 cups all-purpose flour
- 1/2 cup granulated sugar
- 1/4 cup brown sugar, packed
- 1 tsp baking powder
- 1/2 tsp baking soda
- 1/4 tsp salt
- 1/2 cup unsalted butter, melted
- 2 large ripe bananas, mashed (about 1 cup)
- 2 large eggs
- 1/2 cup coconut milk (or regular milk)
- 1/2 cup shredded coconut
- 1 tsp vanilla extract

For the Topping (optional):

- 1/4 cup shredded coconut
- 2 tbsp granulated sugar

Instructions:

1. **Prepare the Muffin Batter:**
    - Preheat your oven to 350°F (175°C). Line a muffin tin with paper liners or grease it lightly.
    - In a large bowl, whisk together the flour, granulated sugar, brown sugar, baking powder, baking soda, and salt.
    - In another bowl, mix the melted butter, mashed bananas, eggs, coconut milk, and vanilla extract until well combined.
    - Pour the wet ingredients into the dry ingredients and stir until just combined. Fold in the shredded coconut.
2. **Fill the Muffin Tin:**
    - Divide the batter evenly among the muffin cups, filling each about 2/3 full.
3. **Add Topping (Optional):**
    - In a small bowl, mix the shredded coconut and granulated sugar. Sprinkle this mixture over the tops of the muffins for added texture and sweetness.
4. **Bake:**
    - Bake for 20-25 minutes, or until the muffins are golden brown and a toothpick inserted into the center comes out clean.
5. **Cool:**
    - Allow the muffins to cool in the tin for about 5 minutes before transferring them to a wire rack to cool completely.

Enjoy:

- Enjoy your Banana Coconut Muffins warm or at room temperature!

These muffins are moist and flavorful, combining the sweetness of ripe bananas with the tropical touch of coconut.

Passion Fruit Sorbet with Fresh Mint

Ingredients:

- 1 cup passion fruit juice (fresh or store-bought, with pulp if possible)
- 3/4 cup granulated sugar
- 1 cup water
- 1/4 cup freshly squeezed lime juice
- 1 tbsp finely chopped fresh mint leaves
- Optional: additional mint leaves for garnish

Instructions:

1. **Prepare the Syrup:**
    - In a small saucepan, combine the water and granulated sugar. Heat over medium heat, stirring until the sugar is fully dissolved. Remove from heat and let it cool to room temperature.
2. **Mix the Sorbet Base:**
    - In a large bowl, mix the passion fruit juice, lime juice, and cooled sugar syrup.
    - Stir in the finely chopped fresh mint leaves.
3. **Chill the Mixture:**
    - Refrigerate the mixture for at least 1 hour to chill thoroughly.
4. **Churn the Sorbet:**
    - Pour the chilled mixture into an ice cream maker and churn according to the manufacturer's instructions, usually about 20-25 minutes, until it reaches a soft-serve consistency.
5. **Freeze:**
    - Transfer the sorbet to an airtight container and freeze for at least 2 hours to firm up.
6. **Serve:**
    - Scoop the sorbet into bowls or cones. Garnish with additional fresh mint leaves if desired.

Enjoy:

- Enjoy your refreshing Passion Fruit Sorbet with a hint of fresh mint!

This sorbet is a delightful tropical treat with a vibrant flavor and cooling minty finish.

Tropical Fruit Parfait

Ingredients:

- 2 cups vanilla yogurt (or coconut yogurt for a dairy-free option)
- 1 cup granola
- 1 cup fresh pineapple, diced
- 1 cup fresh mango, diced
- 1 cup fresh strawberries, sliced
- 1/2 cup shredded coconut
- 2 tbsp honey or agave syrup (optional, for drizzling)
- Fresh mint leaves (for garnish, optional)

Instructions:

1. **Prepare the Ingredients:**
    - Wash and prepare the fresh fruit. Dice the pineapple and mango, and slice the strawberries.
2. **Assemble the Parfaits:**
    - In serving glasses or bowls, start by spooning a layer of vanilla yogurt into the bottom.
    - Add a layer of granola over the yogurt.
    - Top with a layer of diced pineapple, mango, and strawberries.
    - Repeat the layers until the glasses or bowls are filled, finishing with a layer of fruit on top.
3. **Add Final Touches:**
    - Sprinkle shredded coconut over the top layer of fruit.
    - Drizzle with honey or agave syrup if desired for extra sweetness.
    - Garnish with fresh mint leaves if using.
4. **Serve:**
    - Serve immediately or refrigerate for up to an hour before serving.

Enjoy:

- Enjoy your refreshing and colorful Tropical Fruit Parfait!

This parfait combines creamy yogurt, crunchy granola, and vibrant tropical fruits for a delicious and healthy treat.

Coconut-Lime Bars

Ingredients:

For the Crust:

- 1 1/2 cups graham cracker crumbs
- 1/4 cup granulated sugar
- 1/2 cup unsalted butter, melted

For the Filling:

- 1 can (14 oz) sweetened condensed milk
- 1 cup shredded coconut
- 1/2 cup freshly squeezed lime juice
- Zest of 2 limes
- 3 large eggs

For the Topping (optional):

- Extra shredded coconut for garnish
- Lime zest for garnish

Instructions:

1. **Prepare the Crust:**
    - Preheat your oven to 350°F (175°C). Line an 8x8-inch baking pan with parchment paper, leaving some overhang for easy removal.
    - In a medium bowl, combine the graham cracker crumbs, granulated sugar, and melted butter. Mix until the crumbs are evenly coated and resemble wet sand.
    - Press the mixture firmly into the bottom of the prepared baking pan to form an even layer.
    - Bake the crust for 10 minutes. Remove from the oven and let it cool slightly.
2. **Prepare the Filling:**
    - In a large bowl, whisk together the sweetened condensed milk, shredded coconut, lime juice, lime zest, and eggs until well combined.
    - Pour the filling over the pre-baked crust and spread it out evenly.
3. **Bake:**
    - Bake for 20-25 minutes, or until the filling is set and the top is lightly golden. The center should be firm but slightly jiggly.
4. **Cool and Chill:**
    - Allow the bars to cool in the pan on a wire rack for about 30 minutes.
    - Once cooled, refrigerate for at least 2 hours or until completely chilled and firm.
5. **Serve:**

- - Once chilled, lift the bars out of the pan using the parchment paper overhang and cut into squares.
  - Garnish with extra shredded coconut and lime zest if desired.

Enjoy:

- Enjoy your zesty and coconutty Coconut-Lime Bars!

These bars are a perfect blend of tart lime and sweet coconut, with a crumbly graham cracker crust. They're great for a refreshing dessert or a sweet treat.

Mango-Pineapple Cupcakes

Ingredients:

For the Cupcakes:

- 1 1/2 cups all-purpose flour
- 1 cup granulated sugar
- 1 1/2 tsp baking powder
- 1/2 tsp baking soda
- 1/4 tsp salt
- 1/2 cup unsalted butter, softened
- 2 large eggs
- 1/2 cup coconut milk (or regular milk)
- 1/2 cup mango puree (fresh or canned)
- 1/2 cup crushed pineapple, drained
- 1 tsp vanilla extract

For the Frosting:

- 1/2 cup unsalted butter, softened
- 1 1/2 cups powdered sugar
- 2 tbsp mango puree
- 1 tbsp crushed pineapple, drained
- 1/2 tsp vanilla extract
- 1-2 tbsp milk or coconut milk (as needed for consistency)

For the Garnish (optional):

- Small pieces of fresh mango
- Shredded coconut

Instructions:

1. **Prepare the Cupcakes:**
   - Preheat your oven to 350°F (175°C). Line a muffin tin with paper liners.
   - In a medium bowl, whisk together the flour, granulated sugar, baking powder, baking soda, and salt.
   - In a large bowl, beat the softened butter until creamy. Add the eggs, one at a time, beating well after each addition.
   - Mix in the coconut milk, mango puree, and vanilla extract until combined.
   - Gradually add the dry ingredients to the wet mixture, mixing until just combined.
   - Gently fold in the crushed pineapple.
2. **Bake the Cupcakes:**

- Divide the batter evenly among the cupcake liners, filling each about 2/3 full.
- Bake for 18-22 minutes, or until a toothpick inserted into the center comes out clean.
- Allow the cupcakes to cool in the pan for 5 minutes, then transfer to a wire rack to cool completely.

3. **Prepare the Frosting:**
   - In a medium bowl, beat the softened butter until smooth.
   - Gradually add the powdered sugar, mixing on low speed until incorporated.
   - Mix in the mango puree, crushed pineapple, and vanilla extract.
   - If the frosting is too thick, add milk or coconut milk, one tablespoon at a time, until you reach the desired consistency.
4. **Frost the Cupcakes:**
   - Once the cupcakes are completely cooled, frost them with the mango-pineapple frosting using a piping bag or a spatula.
5. **Add Garnish (Optional):**
   - Garnish the frosted cupcakes with small pieces of fresh mango and a sprinkle of shredded coconut if desired.

Enjoy:

- Enjoy your tropical Mango-Pineapple Cupcakes!

These cupcakes are a delicious blend of tropical flavors with a moist crumb and creamy frosting, perfect for a sweet treat or special occasion.

Pineapple Coconut Bars

Ingredients:

For the Crust:

- 1 1/2 cups graham cracker crumbs
- 1/4 cup granulated sugar
- 1/2 cup unsalted butter, melted

For the Filling:

- 1 can (14 oz) sweetened condensed milk
- 1 cup shredded coconut
- 1 cup crushed pineapple, drained
- 1/4 cup freshly squeezed lime juice
- 2 large eggs
- 1 tsp vanilla extract

For the Topping (optional):

- Extra shredded coconut for garnish
- Lime zest for garnish

Instructions:

1. **Prepare the Crust:**
   - Preheat your oven to 350°F (175°C). Line an 8x8-inch baking pan with parchment paper, leaving some overhang for easy removal.
   - In a medium bowl, combine the graham cracker crumbs, granulated sugar, and melted butter. Mix until the crumbs are evenly coated and resemble wet sand.
   - Press the mixture firmly into the bottom of the prepared baking pan to form an even layer.
   - Bake the crust for 10 minutes, then remove from the oven and let it cool slightly.
2. **Prepare the Filling:**
   - In a large bowl, whisk together the sweetened condensed milk, shredded coconut, crushed pineapple, lime juice, eggs, and vanilla extract until well combined.
   - Pour the filling over the pre-baked crust and spread it out evenly.
3. **Bake:**
   - Bake for 25-30 minutes, or until the filling is set and the top is lightly golden. The center should be firm but slightly jiggly.
4. **Cool and Chill:**
   - Allow the bars to cool in the pan on a wire rack for about 30 minutes.

        - Once cooled, refrigerate for at least 2 hours or until completely chilled and firm.
5. **Serve:**
        - Once chilled, lift the bars out of the pan using the parchment paper overhang and cut into squares.
        - Garnish with extra shredded coconut and lime zest if desired.

Enjoy:

- Enjoy your Pineapple Coconut Bars with a tropical twist!

These bars are a delicious blend of sweet pineapple and coconut with a buttery graham cracker crust, perfect for a refreshing and easy dessert.

Spiced Banana Cake with Rum Glaze

Ingredients:

For the Cake:

- 1 1/2 cups all-purpose flour
- 1 tsp baking powder
- 1/2 tsp baking soda
- 1/2 tsp salt
- 1/2 tsp ground cinnamon
- 1/4 tsp ground nutmeg
- 1/4 tsp ground cloves
- 1/2 cup unsalted butter, softened
- 1 cup granulated sugar
- 2 large eggs
- 1 cup mashed ripe bananas (about 3 medium bananas)
- 1/2 cup buttermilk (or milk with 1/2 tbsp lemon juice)
- 1 tsp vanilla extract

For the Rum Glaze:

- 1/4 cup unsalted butter
- 1/4 cup dark rum
- 1/4 cup brown sugar, packed
- 1/4 cup heavy cream
- 1/2 tsp vanilla extract

Instructions:

1. **Prepare the Cake:**
   - Preheat your oven to 350°F (175°C). Grease and flour a 9-inch round cake pan or line it with parchment paper.
   - In a medium bowl, whisk together the flour, baking powder, baking soda, salt, cinnamon, nutmeg, and cloves.
   - In a large bowl, cream the softened butter and granulated sugar together until light and fluffy.
   - Add the eggs one at a time, beating well after each addition.
   - Mix in the mashed bananas, buttermilk, and vanilla extract until well combined.
   - Gradually add the dry ingredients to the wet mixture, mixing until just combined.
   - Pour the batter into the prepared cake pan and smooth the top.
2. **Bake:**
   - Bake for 25-30 minutes, or until a toothpick inserted into the center of the cake comes out clean.

- Allow the cake to cool in the pan for 10 minutes, then transfer it to a wire rack to cool completely.

3. **Prepare the Rum Glaze:**
   - In a small saucepan, melt the butter over medium heat.
   - Stir in the dark rum, brown sugar, and heavy cream. Bring to a simmer, stirring constantly until the sugar is dissolved and the glaze has thickened slightly (about 3-5 minutes).
   - Remove from heat and stir in the vanilla extract.
4. **Glaze the Cake:**
   - Once the cake is completely cooled, pour the warm rum glaze over the top, letting it drizzle down the sides.
5. **Serve:**
   - Let the glaze set for a few minutes before slicing and serving.

Enjoy:

- Enjoy your Spiced Banana Cake with a delightful Rum Glaze!

This cake offers a warm, spiced flavor with a rich rum glaze, making it a perfect treat for special occasions or a cozy dessert.

Coconut-Pineapple Macarons

Ingredients:

For the Macaron Shells:

- 1 3/4 cups powdered sugar
- 1 cup almond flour
- 1/2 cup granulated sugar
- 3 large egg whites, room temperature
- 1/4 tsp cream of tartar
- 1/2 tsp vanilla extract
- Yellow food coloring (optional)

For the Coconut-Pineapple Filling:

- 1/2 cup unsalted butter, softened
- 1 cup powdered sugar
- 1/4 cup canned crushed pineapple, drained
- 1/2 cup shredded coconut
- 1/2 tsp vanilla extract

Instructions:

1. **Prepare the Macaron Shells:**
   - Preheat your oven to 300°F (150°C). Line baking sheets with parchment paper or silicone baking mats.
   - In a food processor, blend the powdered sugar and almond flour until fine. Sift the mixture to remove any large bits.
   - In a large bowl, beat the egg whites and cream of tartar with an electric mixer until soft peaks form.
   - Gradually add the granulated sugar, continuing to beat until stiff, glossy peaks form.
   - Gently fold in the sifted powdered sugar and almond flour mixture in thirds until fully incorporated. Add vanilla extract and food coloring if using.
   - Transfer the batter to a piping bag fitted with a round tip. Pipe small circles onto the prepared baking sheets, about 1.5 inches in diameter. Tap the baking sheets on the counter to release air bubbles.
   - Let the piped shells sit at room temperature for about 30 minutes, or until a skin forms on the surface.
2. **Bake the Macaron Shells:**
   - Bake for 15-18 minutes, or until the macarons are set and have a slight "foot" around the edges. Let them cool completely on the baking sheets.
3. **Prepare the Filling:**

- In a medium bowl, beat the softened butter until creamy. Gradually add the powdered sugar and continue to beat until light and fluffy.
- Mix in the drained crushed pineapple, shredded coconut, and vanilla extract until well combined.

4. **Assemble the Macarons:**
    - Once the macaron shells are completely cooled, spread or pipe a small amount of the coconut-pineapple filling onto the flat side of half of the shells.
    - Top with the remaining shells, pressing gently to sandwich the filling.
5. **Serve:**
    - Let the assembled macarons sit for at least 24 hours in the refrigerator to allow the flavors to meld and the filling to soften the shells.

Enjoy:

- Enjoy your tropical Coconut-Pineapple Macarons!

These macarons combine the delicate texture of traditional macarons with the sweet, fruity flavors of coconut and pineapple.

www.ingramcontent.com/pod-product-compliance
Lightning Source LLC
LaVergne TN
LVHW081608060526
838201LV00054B/2147